OXFORD

SATB choir and piano four-hands with optional percussion and string bass

Mack Wilberg

The Virgin Mary had a baby boy

oxford christmas music

The Virgin Mary Had a Baby Boy

For Mixed Choir (SATB) and Piano Four-hands
with Optional Percussion and String Bass

Traditional West Indian Carol;
Mack Wilberg, *arr.*

A full score and set of parts for an alternative orchestral arrangement (piccolo, flute, oboe, clarinet, bassoon, optional trumpets and trombones, steel drums or piano, percussion, and strings) are available on rental from the Publisher.

The Mormon Tabernacle Choir with the Orchestra at Temple Square has recorded Mack Wilberg's orchestral arrangement of *The Virgin Mary Had a Baby Boy* on the CD "Sing Choirs of Angels" (MTC 1063).

© Oxford University Press, Inc. 2006. Assigned to Oxford University Press 2010. Printed in U.S.A.

Vir - gin Ma - ry had a ba - by boy, __ the Vir - gin Ma - ry had a ba - by boy, __ the

25
unis.
div.
T.
B.
He come from the glo - - ry,
He come from the glo-ri-ous King-dom.
Shak.
Cong.
Pno.
Sec.
D.B.
29
S.
A.
mf unis.
The
8va

41
div.
S.
A.
He come from the glo - - ry,
He come from the glo-ri-ous King-dom,
Shak.
Cong.
(8)
Pno.
Sec.
D.B.
45
unis.
div.
S.
A.
He come from the glo - - ry,
He come from the glo-ri-ous King-dom.
Shak.
Cong.
Pno.
Sec.
D.B.

String Bass

THE VIRGIN MARY HAD A BABY BOY

Traditional West Indian Carol;
Mack Wilberg, *arr.*

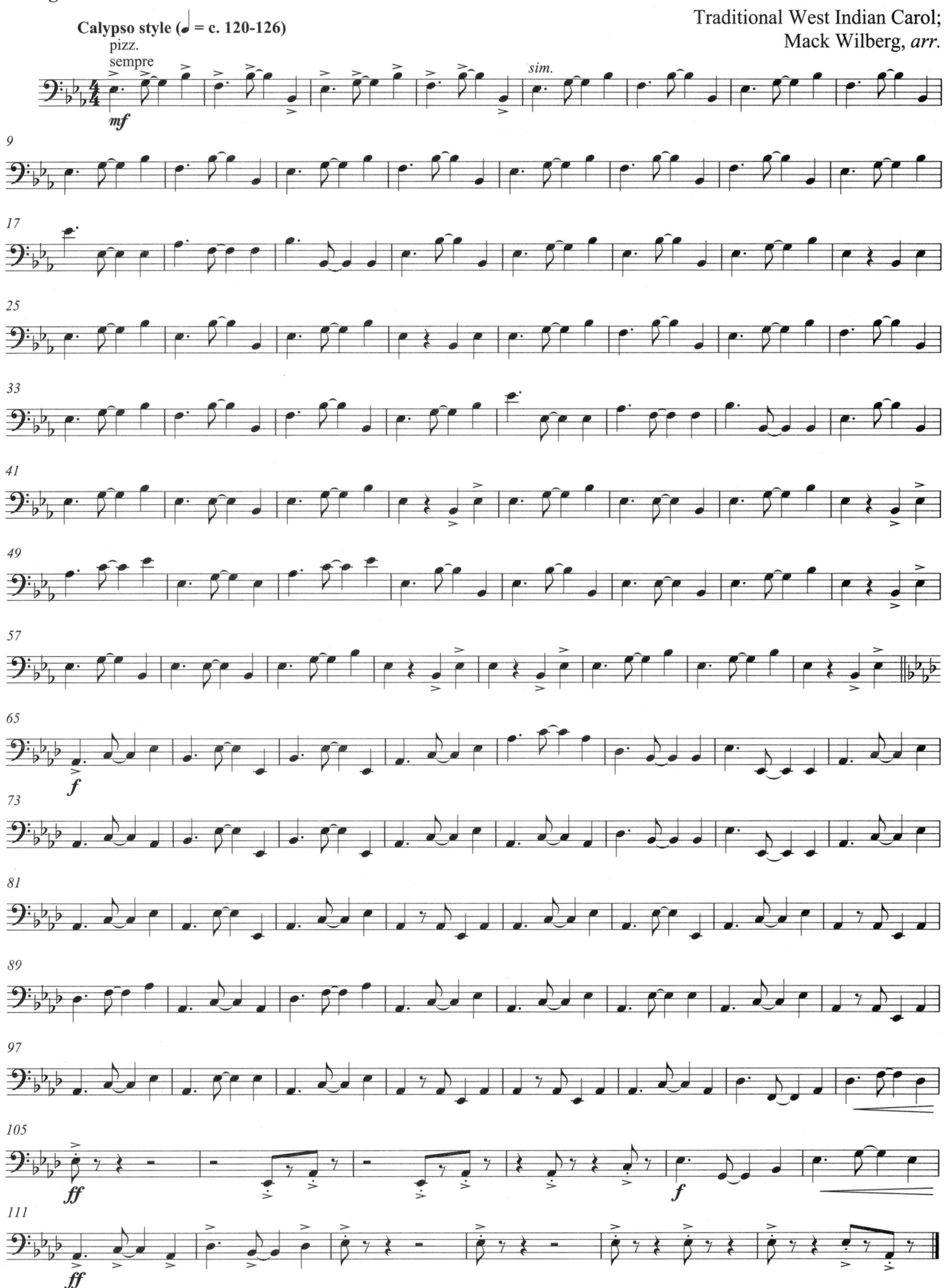

Printed in U.S.A.

Percussion

THE VIRGIN MARY HAD A BABY BOY

Traditional West Indian Carol;
Mack Wilberg, *arr.*

Printed in U.S.A.

Mack Wilberg is the Associate Music Director of the Mormon Tabernacle Choir and the Music Director of the Temple Square Chorale.

He is a former professor of music at Brigham Young University, where he received his bachelor's degree; his master's and doctoral degrees are from the University of Southern California.

In addition to his conducting responsibilities he is active as a pianist, choral clinician, composer, arranger, and guest conductor throughout the United States and abroad. In addition to the many compositions he has written for the Mormon Tabernacle Choir, his works have been performed by artists such as Renée Fleming, Frederica von Stade, Bryn Terfel, The King's Singers, and narrators Walter Cronkite and Claire Bloom.

Wilberg's arrangements and compositions are performed and recorded all over the world. With their grandeur, energy, and craftsmanship, they inspire performers and audiences everywhere.

"Mack Wilberg has emerged as one of the pre-eminent composers and arrangers of choral music in the United States today."

Craig Jessop, Music Director
Mormon Tabernacle Choir

Have you tried?

Still, still, still

Gloria tibi domine

Lullee, lullo, lullai, lullabye

O magnum mysterium

Silent night

How Far Is It To Bethlehem?

oxford christmas music

OXFORD
UNIVERSITY PRESS

www.oup.com

ISBN 978-0-19-386929-5

9 780193 869295